TRAILBLAZER

THE JOURNEY OF BLACK PHYSICIST CARL OLIVER CLARK

BARBARA RANDALL CLARK

Copyright © 2022 Barbara Randall Clark.

All rights reserved. No part of this book may be reproduced, stored, or transmitted by any means—whether auditory, graphic, mechanical, or electronic—without written permission of both publisher and author, except in the case of brief excerpts used in critical articles and reviews. Unauthorized reproduction of any part of this work is illegal and is punishable by law.

ISBN: 979-8-88640-190-5 (sc)
ISBN: 979-8-88640-191-2 (hc)
ISBN: 979-8-88640-192-9 (e)

Because of the dynamic nature of the Internet, any web addresses or links contained in this book may have changed since publication and may no longer be valid. The views expressed in this work are solely those of the author and do not necessarily reflect the views of the publisher, and the publisher hereby disclaims any responsibility for them.

One Galleria Blvd., Suite 1900, Metairie, LA 70001
1-888-421-2397

This biography is dedicated to my children, Carl Robert "Bobby" and Angela Teresa, and to any children born to them as well as family and friends interested in my life history.

Excellence is not just a
gift given, but a skill perfected.

CONTENTS

Foreword 1
Acknowledgments 3
Introduction 5
The Beginning 7
The Poly Technic Experience 15
The Journey Continues 35
The Children 39
Terminal Degree and Advisors 41
Foundation Grants and Programs 45
Coworker Comments 47
Student Comments 51
Awards and Recognitions 55
The Butterfly Effect 59
About the Author 63
About the Layout Artist 65

FOREWORD

Two roads diverged in a wood, and I,
I took the one less traveled by,
And that has made all the difference.

—Robert Frost, "The Road Not Taken"

Dr. Carl Clark's story and legacy is one that needs to be written so that it can inspire future generations of youth. Carl, who has been a close friend and mentor of mine for over thirty-five years, was raised in Baltimore, Maryland, and became the first African American to graduate from poly high school in 1955. By doing this, he helped to integrate and break racial color lines for generations of students that followed him in the Baltimore City Public Schools. His history making did not stop with this because in 1976 he became the first African American to graduate with a PhD in physics from the University of South Carolina. He also had a distinguished teaching and research career at South Carolina State University for thirty-five years. After his retirement, Dr. Clark was an administrator for five years at Morgan State University, his alma mater. Carl is a life member of Alpha Phi Alpha Fraternity, Inc. and his story is a tribute to the men of Alpha everywhere and why I encouraged his wife, Barbara, to write a book about this unique journey.

Dr. Kenneth Mosely

To live peacefully, think of the past with pride,
the future with hope and the present - in the moment!

ACKNOWLEDGMENTS

To my dear wife, Barbara, I give thanks for writing this book about my Poly experience. I would also like to thank my daughter, Angela, the layout artist for this book through default and love. It has been over sixty years since these events first took place, yet many stay still fresh in my mind.

I will instruct thee and teach thee in the way which thou shalt go: I will guide with mine eye. Psalms 32:8

INTRODUCTION

This book is the result of the urgings of fellow Morgan State University Alumni to write an account of the life of my spouse, Carl Oliver Clark. Since he was the first in several areas to accomplish success and open the way for others to follow, it seemed appropriate to record these experiences for his children, his family members, and his friends to know and remember his journey.

THE BEGINNING

Franklin D. Roosevelt served four terms as president of the United States of America (1933–1945) and had three different vice presidents, with Henry Wallace serving as his second VP from 1941 to 1945.

On June 19, 1936, in the last year of the first term of Franklin D. Roosevelt as president of the United States of America, the second son of William Clark and Susan Dowse was born in Savannah, Georgia.

Many were celebrating Juneteenth to commemorate the Texas announcement of the Emancipation Proclamation. The baby was named Carl Oliver, one of six children of the Clark couple. His moniker was a combination of two of his father's friends, Carl Harden (a shoemaker) and Carl Oliver (a postman).

The Extended Family

532 E. Andrews St.

1344 Druid Hill Avenue

Being a close-knit Catholic family, there were relatives abundant to help raise all the children of his parents and his mother Susan's other siblings (Emma and Ellen, twins; Isabelle and Isaac, another set of twins; Frances, Jimmy, and Norma, who died as a baby).

Growing up in Savannah was a joy, and every Sunday, after Mass, the group looked forward to going to Grandmother Susan's house for dinner and to play with all the cousins.

No big effort since they lived next door to his grandmother, where one of Carl's childhood joys was sliding down the banister from upstairs in the Anderson Street house.

With their first three children, Billy, Carl (at age five), and the baby, Anita, his parents moved from Savannah to Maryland, where they lived in West Baltimore on Harlem Avenue for a few months with Mr. and Mrs. Joseph Smith, friends of the family.

Their next move was to 1344 Druid Hill Avenue, and the family attended St. Pious Catholic Church with the children attending Catholic schools.

Lumpkin, GA

Silver Meteor Train

Two years later, his older brother, Billy, and he went to Lumpkin, Georgia, to live with his father's parents and attend schools there. His father was born in Lumpkin and had traveled to Savannah to attend Savannah State College (University), where he met Carl's mother, who was also a student there.

Carl and his brother, Billy, enjoyed the train rides on the Seaboard Air Line Railway and the Silver Meteor Train. It took all day to go from Maryland to Savannah and then a second day to go from Savannah to Lumpkin because of the number of stops along the way.

841 Washington St.

Two years later, the boys left Lumpkin and returned to Maryland, when their father had completed serving two years in the army. East Baltimore, on 841 Washington Street, then became home for the rest of his youth. Another sister, Francis was born in 1943. Two brothers were born, Johnny in 1944 and Jimmy in 1946 to complete the six Clark siblings.

His dad opened a shoe shop, and the four boys of the family were expected to work in his shop while the two girls assisted at home with his mother after she stopped working as an elementary school teacher's aide.

Carl tried other jobs, like working at a catering business, as an assistant in a drugstore, and working with Mr. Tobias, a Jewish merchant, who owned a men's clothing store, to avoid working in the shoe shop.

Baltimore Poly Technic Institute

Marshall A. Levin

Thurgood Marshall

THE POLY TECHNIC EXPERIENCE

Baltimore Poly Technic Institute (BPI), formerly Baltimore Manual Training School, is a US public high school founded in 1883. Though established as an all-male trade school, it now is an institution teaching mathematics, the sciences, and engineering. Most Baltimore city schools were not integrated until after 1954. BPI, an all-male and all-white school, had an unusually advanced and difficult college engineering preparatory curriculum or advanced college preparatory program, otherwise known as the A course, with subjects not offered in the black schools in the city.

Baltimore City leaders supported the "separate but equal" standard that had existed since before it was made law in 1896. They suggested a similar program be set up at the all-black Frederick Douglass High School at a cost of $78,000, a substantial amount of money at that time. A pilot was then suggested that a certain number of Negro students be admitted to Poly's A-course program.

The support for the Poly pilot was boosted by elegant arguments from Marshall Levin (a future circuit judge), representing the Baltimore Urban League, and future Supreme Court Justice Thurgood Marshall, representing the powerful local branch of the NAACP, resulting in many discussions and debates.

The Coordinating Committee on Polytechnic Admissions

16 | BARBARA RANDALL CLARK

The Coordinating Committee on Polytechnic Admissions approached the counselors in the Negro schools to identify students who might qualify for admission to the Poly A-course program. Mrs. Lyons, the counselor at Paul Laurence Dunbar High School, spoke to Carl, his brother Billy, and Gene Giles. Letters were sent to parents to attend the school board hearings.

Carl recalls his mother's attendance at the meetings.

> My mother attended the school board hearings. She talked about the issues presented both in favor and against the enormous change coming. She was impressed by the eloquence of Thurgood Marshall's argument. His concern was they could open a program at Douglas, but would it have the same impact as Poly's because of the history and the tradition of excellence. She came back excited and told us what had happened. Little did she know the full impact of that meeting until much later. The press knew when it happened but there was very little printed. In fact, our pictures weren't printed until almost two years later.

Originally, fifteen students were tapped to participate. However, two students dropped out.

BOARD RULES NEGROES CAN ENTER POLY

5-To-3 Vote Clears Way For Them To Enroll In Famed 'A' Course

Poly Board Member Walter Sondheim, Jr.

Schoolboard Voted 5 To 3 To Open Polytechnic Institute

After several meetings, the Poly Board, including Walter Sondheim Jr., voted 5–3 against the Douglas option, clearing a way to admit the students to Baltimore's Poly A pilot program.

Poly's leaders then took a small step toward ending segregation on its own by selecting the thirteen young black males—three sophomores and ten freshmen to participate in the Poly A course, a program so rigorous and so respected that its graduates enrolled at colleges as sophomores.

Carl, a sophomore at Dunbar High School at age sixteen in 1952, was one of the thirteen males chosen to pilot the Poly A course program—two years before the nationwide 1954 *Brown v. Board of Education* decision was to be implemented.

The other twelve students were Carl's brother William Clark, Leonard Cephas, Milton Cornish, Clarence Daly, Victor Dates, Alvin Giles, Bucky Hawkins, Linwood Jones, Edward Savage, Everett Sherman, Robert Young, and Silas Young. During the summer, before entering Poly, all ten freshmen were tutored for forty hours a week, aimed at making up the gap in their education.

Carl Clark, third from the left on the back row, in the 1953 Poly Yearbook as part of the Mathematics Club.

The three sophomores later joined them to take and pass tests (mostly math) to prepare them for the change. The head of then Morgan State College's English Department (later Morgan State University) also tutored the thirteen each Saturday on writing and English composition. Finally, they had to get parental permission and creditable recommendations before entering as sophomores and freshmen and placed in Poly's A course.

On September 8, 1952, thirteen Black students enrolled in Poly's A-course program.

They knew that their lives would change forever, that the weight of the world would be on their shoulders, and that they would face loneliness and cruelty often, but they welcomed the challenge and did not want to fail. Segregation was in its prime, and those were trying times.

Carl was a member of the Math Club and Craftsman Club and tried out for the Cross-Country Track Team. However, he already worked for a neighborhood pharmacist, and with his focus mainly on his schoolwork, extracurricular activities were limited and not options.

CARL OLIVER CLARK. Advanced College Preparatory Course; Craftsman Club, 2; Mathematics Club, 2, 3, 4; Poly Follies, 4.

109

He states that his best experience was being part of the math club, as one of the top math students, solving problems and discussing new concepts of math.

During a history class, one teacher asked the class to discuss the issue of segregation and the recent Supreme Court decision of *Brown v. the Board of Education*.

Carl vividly recalls this discussion in detail.

> The class began to discuss the pros and cons of the impact of that decision. Some students had serious reservations of how it would work and cause disruptions in the class. This discussion went on for almost the entire class period, going back and forth about the manifestations of the process. Before the end of the class, the instructor noticed that I hadn't commented. He said, "Mr. Clark, what are your feelings about the situation?" I replied, "I have trouble understanding why they say it will not work. Because it is already working very well here." And then the bell rang, dismissing class.

Within three years, Carl completed the Poly A course, graduating in 1955 as Poly's first African American student. However, his English teacher failed him in his senior year, which prevented him from marching with his class. He then had to take a summer school course in English at City College (a rival all-boys school to Poly).

Carl was placed in an advanced class at City and passed with flying colors with a grade of A before he could receive his diploma. Being at Poly (an all-male school, which did not admit females until the 1970s) was, indeed, a unique experience for he consumed the indifference shown him, which then became a part of his persona.

His most disappointing experience was when he was given the failing grade in English (when he knew he had not failed) and he could not march with his class.

> I had this English teacher, and looking back, he was probably pretty prejudiced. I didn't let that hold me back. That's water under the bridge now. My parents accepted it, but they were probably a little hurt because there was no big moment. I was a little hurt too.

Carl would not acknowledge the many prejudices he experienced because he was intent on being successful, and it was of no significance to him to be ignored because he was a black student. He admits to one incident in his junior year, where the prom would have been cancelled if he had chosen to go since the Lord Baltimore Hotel, which hosted the affair, would not admit blacks.

Carl chose not to attend the Poly prom and instead went to the prom at Dunbar.

Wilmer A. DeHuff

Clark reports having made friends at Poly who treated him fairly at school and seemed genuine. They all had one common goal: "a dream that their inner-city school could provide the best education in the state of Maryland for them." There were no protests in 1952 when the first thirteen black students entered Poly, but in 1954, when the *Brown v. Board of Education* decision was being implemented, Poly experienced its first mob of three hundred protesters with signs, name-calling, threats, and insults.

He does recall having supportive classmates protecting him when they had to pass through the mob of protesters as they were going to lunch outside Poly. The crowd let them through without incident, and upon their return, the Poly students who had joined the crowd were threatened with suspension by Principal Wilmer DeHuff if they did not immediately return to class. Student protesters flew back to class, and it turned out to be a one-day experience.

Things appeared integrated inside the school, but outside Poly, Carl could not socialize with students or staff at all, which was the most startling experience of all for him.

Gene Giles as part of the Poly Basketball Team in 1953

Gene Giles, one of the first thirteen students, made the Poly junior varsity football and varsity basketball teams and was embraced by the white players for teaching them his up-tempo style of basketball—a contrast to the methodical game they had played.

There were some schools that refused to play them because they had this black player, and of course he had to endure the negative name-calling. After one year and because he had failed algebra, Giles returned to Dunbar, where, he said, the black students shunned him and there was no encouraging embracement from the NAACP, which to him, both incidences, were disappointing.

Because of the strenuous workload at Poly, Billy Clark, Carl's older brother, also returned to Dunbar. He and Giles graduated from Dunbar High School in 1954.

Among First At Poly

Poly Students with Milton Cornish

one of the best answers to the "unfavorable" letters came from a white Poly student who wrote:

"... I am a Poly boy myself, and I have noticed one significant fact: Amid all the cries and yells that the bottom has fallen out of our social standards, I have yet to hear a complaint from our own student body. We are the ones who have had the best opportunity to arrive at a sensible conclusion. The boys are getting along fine at Poly and I'm sure they will do so in the future.

"If more people would open their minds before they open their mouths, there would be much less controversy over the whole situation."[6]

Pictured from top left, Milton Cornish, Jr., Linwood Jones, Victor Dates and Silas Young

Milton Cornish, one of the ten freshmen of the original thirteen students, admitted that the Poly experience took its toll on the young men.

According to the *Baltimore Sun* article from 2002, he recalls a program featuring a minstrel show that he and classmate Clarence Daly (who recently transitioned in 2013) walked out of after taking as much of the performance as they could. He stated that there were exacting times as well as some lonely experiences and burned-out feelings.

After graduating from Poly, he decided against college and joined the Army Corps of Engineers. He and four of the original ten freshmen graduated from Poly in 1956.

Carl, on the other hand, said he enjoyed the experience and would do it again if given the chance. It is obvious that he enjoyed the challenge, for to be in an environment that renders you invisible because of your color, to feel totally lost and last to be picked for team sports, and to be a symbol or object of hate, all have to leave some painful memories.

Under such circumstances, one develops a total cloak of indifference. Yet for those who succeeded, it seemed a good feeling knowing they carried the torch forward for generations to come.

Milton Cornish and Carl Clark

A salute to the thirteen Blacks who integrated Polytechnic Institute in Baltimore, MD, in 1952.

THE MORING OF THEIR LIFE

Quietly, like falling snow,
Came the morning of their lives
Prepared to meet their subtle foe
Saying daily prayers
To sustain them in their war of diversity
Facing killing fields of
Taunts and stares,
Denials and put downs,
Oppression and subtle assaults
On their intellect and talents
Yet, they survived and succeeded
Grew and produced
With the edge of doubt
Still etched on their souls
The fear of terror still touching their hearts
But the love of God
Still pulling them forward
For they knew they were paving the way for others
And that they would find joy
In the evening of their lives.

Barbara Randall Clark

THE JOURNEY CONTINUES

After Poly, in September of 1955, Carl enrolled at Morgan State University where he earned a bachelor's degree in physics in 1958.

It was in the spring of 1956 that Carl pledged the Beta Alpha Chapter of Alpha Phi Alpha Fraternity, Inc. at Morgan State University, and in December 1956, he became an Alpha man, where he has been an active member for nearly sixty years.

In 1960, he earned a master's degree in physics from Howard University, which was bestowed upon him in 1961 while he was working at Bennett College in Greensboro, North Carolina, during the first of two summers where he taught physics.

In the fall of 1960, Carl began his teaching career at South Carolina State College (now University) as an assistant professor of physics and in 1961 attained the position of associate professor.

Ebony Magazine, 1961, page 117

Barbara as a model in California.

The Bride and Groom June 11, 1966

In 1961, *Ebony* magazine interviewed a broad sample of marriageable males involved in various professions with different opinions for choosing a mate. Carl (at age twenty-four) was chosen as one of the sixty-three most eligible bachelors and one of the forty-nine who had never been married.

In 1962, Donald Coleman, a classmate from Morgan, reintroduced him to another classmate, Barbara Randall, a chemistry major and mathematics minor from Macon, Georgia. For several years, she had worked as a research chemist at the Baltimore Branch of the National Institutes of Health (NIH). After dating for a year, Carl proposed marriage in 1964.

Also in 1964, Carl was granted a leave of absence from South Carolina State College (University) to accept a National Science Foundation Faculty Fellowship at the University of Oregon (Eugene, Oregon) to work on his PhD degree.

Carl and Barbara were married on June 11, 1966 and returned to Orangeburg, where he resumed his teaching duties at South Carolina State College as an assistant professor of physics.

THE CHILDREN

Carl and Barbara became parents of two children: Carl Robert (Bobby), in 1967, and Angela Teresa, in 1969.

Because they lived in faculty housing on the campus of South Carolina State College (University), the children were reared in an academic environment with many opportunities to be involved in educational activities as well as to mingle with all types of cultures.

They both attended Felton Laboratory School, located on the university campus, beginning their formal education at the age of three and graduating from the eighth grade. They both attended Orangeburg-Wilkinson High School.

College for Bobby was Clemson University, graduating with a degree in computer science, where he has been employed since 1990. He married Jennifer Brown of Columbia, South Carolina, on December 13, 1997.

Angela attended South Carolina State University. She spent a year traveling with Up with People before graduating with a dual degree in theater and business. She has been performing all over the world since 1988.

Dr. Charles P. Poole, Jr.

Dr. Horacio A. Farach

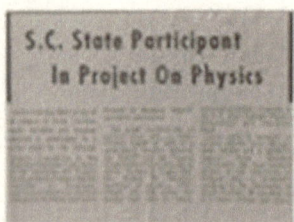
S.C. State Participant In Project On Physics

TERMINAL DEGREE AND ADVISORS

Carl was also a teaching assistant at the University of SC from 1972 to 1974 and continued working on requirements for his PhD in physics, under the leadership of Dr. Charles P. Poole Jr. and Dr. Horacio A. Farach. On one of Carl's first days at the University of SC, Dr. Shutte said to him, "Carl, are you on scholarship?" Carl said, "No sir." Dr. Schutte replied, "Well, come see me on Thursday, and I'll fix that."

> Clark was a student of mine and Dr. Poole's long ago, but still I remember him mostly for his wonderful spirit. He was ready to help any student, not only his partners but also the undergraduate students.
>
> It is easy to remember; he was the best teaching assistant that I had in all forty-two years of my teaching. Carl was among the best but outstanding in reliability. I was always able to count on him upfront with any teaching emergency.
>
> On several occasions, I visited his home and met his family. His beautiful wife writes poetry and read some for us.
>
> All in all, he was a good student in a very difficult field, an outstanding teaching assistant, and a gentleman in every sense of the word. It was a pleasure to be his professor and, now, his friend. (Dr. Horacio A. Facach)

There were many times when we traveled to Columbia to attend social gatherings with both the Poole and Farach families. They, in turn, enjoyed visits to our home and attended activities in Orangeburg.

In 1976, Carl became the first African American to receive his PhD in physics from the University of South Carolina (Columbia, South Carolina).

In 1977, Carl became a full professor at South Carolina State College (University), and in 1988, he was named chairman of the Department of Natural Sciences at South Carolina State College (University).

In 1984, the American Association of Physics Teachers honored Dr. Carl O. Clark at its winter meeting in San Antonio, Texas, with a Distinguished Service Award for his contributions to the teaching and popularization of physics over his teaching years.

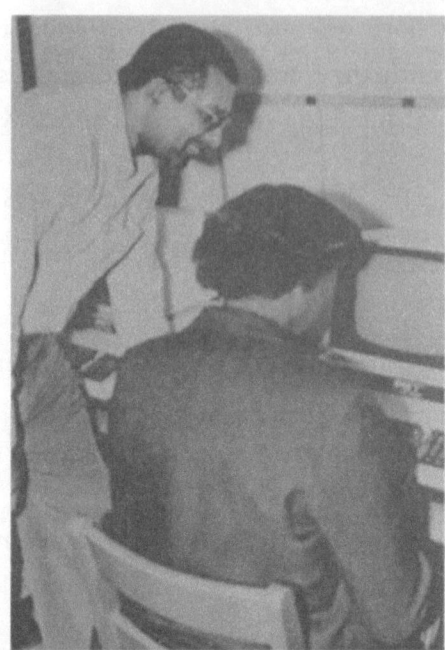

First Kenan Participants

First row left to right
1. Miss Valinda Ray, mathematics teacher 2. Mrs. Barbara Glover, science teacher
3. Cassondra Simmons 4. Arlette Mooore 5. Adriane Maybanks 6. Shauna Patterson
7. Tonya Woodberry 8. Toi Reid 9. Dr. Carl O. Clark, Project Director
10. Dr. Lewie C. Roache, Dean of School of Arts and Sciences

Second row
1. Beth Howard 2. Roidale France 3. Yolanda Keller 4. Barrone Williams 5. Angela Rhodes
6. Rosa Murph 7. Deidre Hutson

Third row
1. Randall Harris 2. Darrell K. Davis 3. Christopher Williams 4. Eddie Haigler
5. Stacy Jones 6. Eric Smalls

Fourth row
1. Charles Butler 2. Carlton Makins, Lab Assistant 3. Martin Roache 4. Nathaniel Cleckley
5. Adrian Glover

FOUNDATION GRANTS AND PROGRAMS

Carl received research grants from the National Science Foundation and the USDA. He also served as director of grants on microcomputers as laboratory instruments in science and basic skills from the Department of Education and from the Kenan Foundation.

Clark has also served as a consultant at Howard University in their cooperative physics program and as a lecturer in other minority institution exchange programs. He was a member of the advisory committee on the project for revitalization of physics teaching at twenty small colleges and became a full member of the Sigma Xi: the Scientific Research Society in 1986.

Carl was the first professor to provide a summer enrichment program using computers for feeder students from local high schools to upgrade achievement in mathematics, reading, science, English, and problem solving. Another objective of the program was to facilitate the students involved in selecting science, mathematics, and technology as a major course of study.

Dr. Judith Salley Guydon

COWORKER COMMENTS

Reflections are from Dr. Judith Salley Guydon during her work with Dr. Carl O. Clark, who was the Kenan project director at South Carolina State University when she arrived in 1983. They worked together until he retired in 1995.

Dr. Guydon reports that the Kenan Foundation project was the first grant-appropriated program that was a partnership between an urban and a rural school district to prepare students in the STEM areas of science, technology, engineering, and math and designed to transition the students from middle school into their ninth-grade year. The program was funded by the Kenan Foundation, now the Kenan Institute at Duke University, with Orangeburg School District Five (urban) and Bowman School District Three (rural) as the first participants in South Carolina. Dr. William Brown of Atlanta, Georgia, served as the project consultant.

Students came to campus for a two-week experience, including SAT prep, and lived in the dorms on campus. There were master teachers in the program in English, math, and science, and after-school tutorials were designed to help the students with college prep course at their high schools after the summer project. Parents were also taught how to read test scores to help students focus on how to study to improve and support them when classes became challenging. Teachers attended national conferences and reviews annually.

The Kenan Foundation was a national program with partner programs on additional college campuses, including North Carolina A&T University, Jackson State University, Dillard University, Bethune-Cookman University, and South Carolina State University.

The Kenan Foundation grant was the forerunner to the Lucile Packard programs and the SCAMP programs at SC State University. These programs were designed to prepare entering freshmen for college-level classes, including science and engineering, and served as a forerunner to computerizing the department. Dr. Clark was the first to introduce "state of the art" technology to the Natural Sciences Department. He was known as the "Apple guy," including Mac computers in a time when other people were using IBM or other PCs.

> I knew Dr. Clark before he became the chair of the Department of Natural Sciences at South Carolina State College (now University). When he became the chairman of the Department of Natural Sciences, he was the only African American physicist for more than fifteen years, until Dan Smith joined the faculty. He was also the principal investigator for the SCAMP grant in 1992 and wrote the first SCAMP grant for the university. I became chair of the Biology Department in 1994, the year before Dr. Clark retired (after thirty-five years at SCSU) and went to chair the Physics Department at Morgan State University in Baltimore. It was those types of stellar programs and his phenomenal "grantmanship" that increased the enrollment in the STEM areas of the university. It was because of his leadership and diligence that South Carolina State University was able to not only pursue and sustain these students but to also retain and matriculate them as well.
>
> In addition to his magnificent academic achievements for the university, Dr. Clark poured his heart and love into the

young men he advised as faculty advisor for the Beta Delta Chapter of Alpha Phi Alpha Fraternity, Inc. Serving for more than fifty years, he has molded and shaped the lives of so many outstanding young men not only on the collegiate level but also training others to follow in his footsteps as an advisor like Mr. Nathaniel Gant, another outstanding former member of our faculty.

His passion for students was hard to surpass, and he loved his students. The quality of life for students was his utmost importance, for he wanted them to not only be intellectually gifted but to see the impact of their commitment to serving the community. So much so that each year, they not only excelled and received the annual trophy for academic achievement but also for community service hours as well, providing the most time to projects in the community and on campus.

I was proud and privileged to be named the chair of the Department of Biological Sciences and to succeed him in 1995 after his retirement. He was my mentor in every sense of the word but also my big brother when I was green behind the ears. He pulled me in as a confidant and became part of my family. We were known as the Mutt and Jeff of science, and almost every time you saw Carl, you saw Judy. I never minded and was honored with the nickname. We had an unorthodox way of working, and we understood that we stayed on the job until the job was done. Every tick of the clock was hit at some point while we were working on one project or another. He poured a lot of care into our lives: dedication, passion, and a drive for excellence. I can only hope that I am holding up his legacy half as well. He is an endeared friend who might have left us (this university) physically, but his impression and commitment will always be with us.

I still expect him to come walking down the hall with a coffee cup in his hand. He will always be one of my dearest friends. (Dr. Judith Salley Guydon)

Dr. Clark gave me one of my very first jobs on the campus of Hodge Hall at South Carolina State College. He was my mentor and encouraged me to continue my education. He always had a heart of gold, and I could not have asked for a better boss. (Kim N. Roper)

STUDENT COMMENTS

His influence on his many students and young Alpha men is extensive, as is evidenced by his many fraternal and teaching awards. In 1987, he received Outstanding Service Awards from the Pi Alpha Chapter (Clemson University) and the Beta Delta Chapter (South Carolina State University) of Alpha Phi Alpha Fraternity, Inc. In that same year, he was presented the Green Award (for Meritorious Service) from the Delta Zeta Lambda (Orangeburg Alumni) Chapter of Alpha Phi Alpha Fraternity, Inc.

> Starting in March 1991, a true friendship began to develop. From the many conversations we had in Hodge Hall, to the periodic pizza socials we had, to the occasional invitations for the chapter to go over to his house for a cookout and share cold refreshments. Once Dr. Clark got to know you, he would always take time to be a mentor. I think it was Summer School in 1991 when I took Physics II under Dr. Clark. It was hard but I survived!
>
> After graduating, I obtained a commission in the United States Coast Guard serving thirteen years. Along the way, I obtained two masters degrees and am now an IT specialist in the US Department of Treasury.
>
> So, Dr. Clark, you will never know how you impacted so many of us that got to know you. I will always hold on

to the life lessons you shared. Many blessings! (Robert Mitchell, Beta Delta, Spring 1991)

To this day, I still credit Dr. Clark as the reason I understand physics and graduated *on time*. He was a good friend, a good Alpha mentor and always encouraged the young men. Plus, he always had the funniest sense of humor when it was needed most. I have lots of great memories of a great man. (Vernon Craig, SC State University, class of 92, Beta Delta, fall 1989)

I remember meeting you in 1987 just before my freshman year at SCSU. SC State had a program that allowed new students to get a jump-start on science and engineering. Your use of Apple computers then was inspiring and ahead of its time. Many of us in the program didn't realize how advanced it was until later in life.

As I worked on campus for Dr. Donald Small, we often visited you to learn about the latest Apple computer technology. I was also in your physics class, and you inspired many of us to be involved more in science and use technology to aid us. We learned a lot about computers during those days thanks to your forward thinking. Thank you for being an inspiring role model. (Steven V. Jennings, SC State University, class of '92)

There are so many great things I could say about Dr. Carl Clark. He was a great mentor, father figure, strong leader, solid professor, fraternity brother and friend to me. Dr. Clark truly had an open-door policy and anything you shared with him stayed between you, him and God. He was never too tired to help me with my homework or what I thought was a life crisis at that time. Dr. Clark was great at sharing his knowledge and wisdom with me and my Beta Delta chapter brothers as we journeyed through collegiate life and into outstanding Alpha men. (Gregory A. Freeman, Beta Delta, fall 1982)

Carl speaking at 2005 Poly

AWARDS AND RECOGNITIONS

On November 18, 2006, he was awarded Alpha's Living Legend Award, celebrating one hundred years of existence of the fraternity for outstanding leadership and service in Alpha Phi Alpha from all the South Carolina chapters of Alpha Phi Alpha Fraternity, Inc.

In 1995, Carl received an award of appreciation for decades of dedication and service from his one thousand students involved in the Kenan Project, Project Access, the Lucile Packard program, and the SCAMP programs.

In May of 1995, after thirty-five years at South Carolina State University, Clark retired and returned to Morgan State University to serve as chairman of the physics department and, later, as assistant dean of the School of Mathematics and Physics, retiring, again, from Morgan State University in 2000 and returning to Orangeburg, South Carolina.

Carl was the first president of the chartered alumni chapter of Morgan State University for the South Atlantic Region, June 16, 2001. This region includes alumni from the states of South Carolina and Augusta and Savannah, Georgia.

Kevin Tolson, Carl Clark and Sam McLaughlin

Robert Young, Clarence Daly, Milton Comish, Carl Clark and Gene Giles

In 2004, after fifty-plus years later, Carl was selected to the Poly Hall of Fame, and in 2005, he returned to Poly to accept the school's Distinguished Alumni Award and speak at its graduation. In June 2012, he was again the commencement speaker at Poly's graduation.

In 2010, two Poly students did a historical documentary of the first thirteen students' experiences and presented it to the Reginald F. Lewis Museum of Maryland African American History and Culture.

Five of the original thirteen students were present and honored. (*From left to right*: Robert Young, Clarence Daly, Milton Cornish, Carl Clark, and Gene Giles).

Still an active member of Alpha Phi Alpha Fraternity, Inc. as part of the Delta Zeta Lambda Alumni Chapter of Orangeburg, South Carolina, he has influenced many of his fellow fraternity brothers.

> There are so many wonderful things to be said about Dr. Clark. What I enjoy the most about him is he is a man of great wisdom and understanding, very dedicated to Alpha, always supportive of our activities and events, encouraging and fostering open communication between brothers, young and old. Dr. Clark lives by the principles of Alpha: manly deeds, scholarship, and love for all mankind. He has always taken a leadership role and always involved all brothers in activities by utilizing all their talents. Stay strong, my brother. (Bo Gathers, former president of Delta Zeta Lambda)

Nick Edwards and Dr. Carl O. Clark

THE BUTTERFLY EFFECT

In finalizing the effect of the butterfly wings that Carl set in motion years ago, we must reference Andy Andrews' book *The Butterfly Effect*. Carl joins the historic group of people whose life decisions and actions changed the world.

Andrew writes that during the Civil War, a Union Army colonel, Joshua Lawrence Chamberlain, gave an order during a battle "to charge" the Confederate army. He had only a few men left with very little reinforcements, but his decision led to the capture of hundreds of enemy soldiers and paved the way for the United States to exist as it does today.

A farmer named Moses Carver lived in a slave state with his wife, Susan. Moses was attacked by psychopaths called Quantrill Raiders, who terrorized and burned his property, shot many people, and dragged off Mary Washington and her sick infant son. Susan, Moses's wife and a friend to Mary, organized a campaign and secured an audience for her husband to meet with the bandits, where he traded his only horse for the sick, naked, almost-dead baby George Washington. Then, for miles, Moses walked through the night with the baby next to his body until he returned home. He and Susan raised the child as their own and promised him an education to honor his deceased mother and gave the baby their name, Carver.

Later, George Washington Carver, as a nineteen year-old honor student at Iowa State University, took the then six year-old Henry Wallace with him on many weekend "botanical expeditions," instilling in him a love for plants and a vision for what plants could do for humanity. This is the same Carver who developed three hundred items from the peanut and eighty-eight things from the sweet potato.

Before Henry Wallace became vice president of the United States, under President Franklin D. Roosevelt, he was the secretary of agriculture and he used his power to create a station in Mexico to hybridize corn and wheat for arid climates, for which he hired Norman Borlaug to run. This work, which saved the lives of more than two billion people, won Borlaug the Nobel Prize and the Presidential Medal of Freedom.

This sequence of events gives proof that everything we do does matter and has an effect on others' actions and choices, for each of us has been born to make a difference—unique and individualized in spirit, thoughts, and feelings, unlike anyone else on earth.

Our lives, predetermined before birth, cannot be packed away, saved for later, or changed, for many unborn generations' lives will be shaped by the actions and choices we now make.

Carl's decision to join thirteen young men to participate in a pilot program to desegregate an all-white boys' school in Baltimore, Maryland, in 1952, opened the door for many young boys (and girls, now) to obtain a better education and pursue a different course in life. One such exceptional student was Nick Edwards, who graduated from Poly in 2012.

Facing many health issues now in his retirement, Carl has reduced and limited his social activities. He still enjoys participation with his fraternity, his card club, and his birthday club.

In the event of his death, Carl has willed his body to science through the Medical University of South Carolina.

Note: Dr. Carl O. Clark lived an additional three years after the publication of the book, Trailblazer. His wife and many others served as care givers. He died on 8/8/17 at age 81.

Daughter (Angela, the layout artist) and (Mother, Barbara (author)

ABOUT THE AUTHOR

Barbara Ann Randall Clark (born in Macon, Georgia) is a retired educator, professional counselor, and presenter with a BS in chemistry/math (MSU/Baltimore), an MEd in counselor/education (SCSU), and a specialist degree (SCSU and USC). One of her four brothers is her twin (Glenn Mason Randall). Her parents, sister, two oldest brothers, and her baby brother are deceased. She and her spouse, Carl, "the Trailblazer," are the parents of two children: Carl Robert (Bobby) and Angela Teresa. A fifty-plus-year member of Delta Sigma Theta Sorority Inc., she was honored as one of the seventy-five Delta Diamonds in 1988 and continues to be an active member of the Orangeburg Alumnae Chapter. She was the 1993 SC Counselor of the Year and was one of ten poets invited to read poetry at Piccolo Spoleto in 2002 (Charleston, South Carolina). Her volunteer involvements include the Special Needs and Disabilities Foundation Board, Meals on Wheels, the Edisto Habitat for Humanity, the Orangeburg Adult Literacy Council Board, and the Orangeburg Community of Character and mentoring at both Brookdale and Mellichamp Elementary Schools. She's a notary public, a member of the Orangeburg Chamber of Commerce and the Holy Trinity Catholic Church. She also holds membership in the Risky Women Investment Group (RWIG), the Orangeburg Red Hatters, the Alpha Wives, and the PNS Real Estate Partnership. She has authored twelve books and coauthored one book for elementary children with Frank Martin. *The Trailblazer* is her fourteenth book. Her website is www.thepoetsnook.net.

Train up a child in the way he should go:
and when he is old, he will not depart from it.

Proverbs 22:6

ABOUT THE LAYOUT ARTIST

Performing in national corporate commercials since the age of four, Angela T. Clark was born in Orangeburg, South Carolina, and has a dual degree in theater and business from South Carolina State University. Angela is the first African American woman to hold the titles of Miss North Charleston, SC Queen of Roses, and Miss Orangeburg County, all within the Miss South Carolina/Miss America Scholarship Organization. Since 1988 she has performed as featured headliner and singer in over seventy countries, most recently performing in Italy, Greece, Turkey, Monaco, and Morocco.

Currently the president/founder and local executive director of the CROWN Group, a marketing and professional development agency that sponsors the Miss Orangeburg County, Miss Florence, Miss Wilson, Miss Orangeburg County Teen, Miss Garden City Teen, and Miss Florence Teen Pageant, Angela is currently pursuing her MBA in entrepreneurship at South Carolina State University.

Note: Our daughter, Angela Teresa Clark, the layout artist of the book, Trailblazer, died silently, in her sleep, on 7/4/21 at age 52.